I0140491

Single Mother On the M.O.V.E.

LaShandaFaye Books & Publishing

Copyright © 2011 LaShanda Faye
All rights reserved.

ISBN: 0-6155-6277-9
ISBN-13: 9780615562773

Single Mother On the M.O.V.E.

"Are You One?"

LaShanda Faye

Dedication

This book is dedicated to all the single mothers in the world. It is writ-ten from a single mother's perspective. I want all single mothers, young and old, of all colors, creeds, and nations to enjoy this book and be enriched by what it says.

Table of Contents

.

Introduction

Are you fulfilling your dreams and goals in life while being a single mother? Are you traveling to that special place you've always desired to travel to with and without your children? Are you pursuing, starting the business of your dreams or the career of your choice? Not just working a job you don't enjoy just to make ends meet, but going after what seems impossible right now, because of the responsibility you carry daily as a single mother? Maybe you believe you should change your geographical location, move out of the city or state you've lived in your whole life, but you've been so afraid to move because of fear of what might or might not happen. If this sounds like you, what or who is stopping you from achieving these things you so desire? I'll tell you who—you!

Sometimes deep down inside we may have negative thoughts about ourselves, so that we really don't believe we can fulfill the dreams and goals we have or once had. We may have even forgotten them because of the myriad of responsibilities we have as a single mother. Our minds are on the cares of this life with our children—having to cook, having to clean, go to school conferences, help with school work—and the list seems to go on and on, we are the one person that hold it all together. Or maybe your a single mother that just can't get it together at all with your children. Somehow or another you never manage to do anything with them, your house seems to always be a mess, maybe you miss conferences, and spend all your time doing what you want to do and are not really concerned about the children at all. They are just too much, so it seems! Some might ignore their children needs completely, totally unaware, and begin to sink into men, drugs, alcohol, gambling, or partying just to numb themselves of the pain and heartache of single-motherhood.

You're not being fulfilled and neither are your children, and yet you don't know how to get a handle on this life you're leading—so you watch other people accomplish their dreams and goals—but when it comes to yourself or your children, you're negative. You just don't believe. You say, "Other people can, but I can't, at least not right now! Or, maybe you look for other people's approval and get sucked into their opinions. If they don't agree with your dreams, you allow what they say to impact you in such a way that it stops you from believing in yourself or your children, so you never go forward and your children never go forward and fulfill what they have a passion for either, because they can only go as far as you push them—and it becomes a never ending cycle from generation to generation. I once fit all of those shoes at some point in my life or another!

But, I have good news for you. There is a way out. You are not alone! Studies show there are 10+ million single mothers in the United States alone. There are plenty of other women who stand in the same position you're in; there is nothing new under the sun or on earth. I repeat—you are not alone! We are standing with you.

I say standing because that's exactly what you're still doing, standing, as long as you have breath in your body and you wake up daily to stand up out of your bed, you have something special to do, something that only you can do. And change is coming to your life. You have a purpose for existing here on earth, it wasn't just to give birth to another human per say, but to give birth to destiny, dreams, visions and desires! You are standing every day through all the circumstances and situations that may have tried to get you down and stop you, but every time single mothers get in a bind and are not sure how we will get out—BAM—(as Emeril says) a blessing shows up and we receive what we need in that situation at that paticular time.

Before you know it, we will look back over the past years and say, "Hmmm, I made it through! We did not go hungry, the children had shoes to wear, and we had a place to lay our heads at night, even if you were homeless and living in a shelter you still had a place to lay your head." We realize then that we might not have had everything we wanted, but we sure had everything we needed. It all depends on our perception!

This is when you have to realize that there is something bigger than you involved here on earth in your life. There is something outside of your struggle that can keep you stable, and that my sister is God. If you didn't know that, now you know! I encourage you to begin building a relationship with Him if you haven't already and learn the purpose for which he has placed you on this earth. Once you understand that, you will then understand that you have purpose for existing and begin to know in part what your purpose is; you will become more serious about being a *Single Mother On the M.O.V.E.*

chapter

ONE

Change Can Happen

We single mothers must join together and support each other with our children in this day and age. Joining together will make us feel stronger, we will feel less stress, and this will lead to more success with our children. One of the many ways we can join together is to form single mother fellowship groups to share ideas on how to help our children become better people. In these groups, we should explore the many challenges we confront with our children and the solutions we have found to overcome these challenges. We can share the victory in each situation so that other single mothers get ideas of how to face things when they go through similar problems with their children.

Another way we can join together is to call a single mother who has older children than you and listen to their experiences. By doing this we can gather solutions, prepare for what we may have to face or totally change a direction that we may be going in with our child. Our answer to a situation may not always be the best answer. Support for the single mother is crucial, because *"we are single mothers trying to live balanced lives in an imbalanced situation"*, not having a father in the home takes away from Gods original design for the family unit. Many times when we deal with situations alone, they don't always turn out the way we think they should, then in our disappointment, we get depressed and become passive with our children. We end up not setting high enough standards and expectations for them, because we give up on them or lose confidence in our self as an effective or good enough parent, and then when they fall into wrong lifestyle choices, we are humiliated, shocked, and displeased with them, ourselves, and with the world in general. By reaching out to other single mothers for ideas, support, and assistance, we can increase the chances that our children have at being successful in life and making it through all the negative statistics.

My Testimony

My name is LaShandaFaye Hodges, but you can call me Faye. As a child, I had big dreams I wanted to achieve, but somewhere along the way I became a single mother of three children who came from two different fathers. I was a victim of repeated sexual abuse growing up, which is why I was very permiscuous by the time I was old enough to be. I was the child of a father and stepfather (seed of an adulteress situation), neither of whom stuck around to raise me. I was a C average student throughout school and it seemed like everything I tried to do just did not succeed. Everywhere I turned, somehow, some way, rejection was always the outcome. Over time, I became a woman with a criminal background who had committed a wide array of ungodly acts. My problems became deeper and deeper.

If you look at just that small portion of my life, it doesn't look like a set-up for success does it? But let me tell you, success is not in where I've been or what it looks like; it's in where I'm going, what I believe and just the mere fact that I get there. I try not to emphasize the negatives in my life, but some days while going through single motherhood I think, "What if my life would have been different growing up?", or, "If my mother would have done things differently with me when I was growing up, then maybe I wouldn't be going through this now." The bottom line, however, is I am who I am, and I've made the choices that I've made. I can't go back and change them, but I can change how my future will be and how my children's future will be by changing my "what if" negative thinking into "what if" positive thinking;and then take small steps into making those "what if" positive thoughts a reality. Do something productive and positive today to make your "what if" dreams of the future happen. We can't change the past and we definitely can't worry about the future, but we can create a better right now for our lives to have a better future.

On January 16, 1998, when I realized I could not run my own life anymore, I surrendered it to God and asked Him to help me through the power of Jesus Christ, I accepted Jesus in my heart as my personal Lord and Savior and there was an instant change inside of me. I've grown tremendously because of His saving power. Now that doesn't mean I started doing everything right and nothing wrong, but I did begin to develop a relationship with God. I began to go to church and read my Bible to learn about God, to understand who He is and what His standard of living is for me, and as I started to live more like Christ, I began to see a transformation in my attitude and my actions. I began to not want to do the same things I had been doing, because I saw through reading the bible those things displeased God and I saw through reading the bible what pleased God, so I began asking Him to help me change to what He wanted me to be. I wanted to love people more and to display more kindness toward others. A change came over me and this same change awaits you if you have not already experienced it.

If you are not happy with where you are in your life, don't stay unhappy. Get ready to get excited, because a process of change is happening to you right now as you read this book. I've been transformed into a woman who no longer needs a man in her life to complete her. A woman who no longer lowers her standards because she is afraid of loosing the man she has or wants. I'm not the woman who had to get high every day as soon as her feet hit the ground. I'm no longer the woman who always sought out people for company because I never wanted to be home alone. I was always thinking I had to get into something and go somewhere. No longer am I the woman who cared more about everyone's opinion more than my own, or God's. I'm no longer the woman who was always looking for the next party, club, or hangout spot, dropping off my children to sitters, not knowing what was really going to go on with them when I left. I'm changed now, all because of the blood of Jesus Christ and the salvation He made available to the world, you can be too. Yes, I'm now an author of bestselling books nationally and internationally, a woman who has learned to make her own decisions based on dreams and desires which I believe God has placed inside of me. I'm also a mother who is careful with her children. I realize everything is not just all about me.

With all I've shared with you, there is some good and some bad, but through it all I'm still standing! Yes, I took a few hard hits, but I got up and you will too. Nevertheless, if it had not been for my meeting with Jesus Christ, I would not have gotten up.

You know, it seems to me that there are people out there who just seem to have the natural ability to make it without God (so it seems, anyway). It seems like they are just naturally strong and can take whatever comes their way. Then there are others, like me. I am so weak that unless I pray, go to church, and have faith in God, I can't make it. In doing those things, I gain strength, and when I'm strengthened I'm able to thrive. That's when I'm able to be a *Single Mother on the M.O.V.E.*

I wrote this classic book so that you and I could be encouraged and stay encouraged. Nothing is impossible—to the one who believes, all things are possible. When you couple believing in yourself with belief in the dreams and goals God has put inside you, these dreams and goals will be accomplished. Good things will begin to happen in your life and you'll make it through anything you face. Let's go into the book and begin our life- changing journey together.

chapter

TWO

Who is Faye? Is She a Single Mother on the M.O.V.E.?

I graduated from high school in 1992, and I didn't have a clear direction of where I was going or what I was going to do with my life. I always wanted to be a singer, actress, dancer but when that seemed as if it were impossible, I then said that I wanted to graduate from college (after I stopped believing in being involved in the whole arts, and entertainment industry), get a good job, get married, have children, and stay home with the children until they went to school all day, then I'd return to work (you know the whole American dream picket fence thing, hah, right). Well, my life did not go that way.

I very seldom received affirmation by the important people in my life while growing as a child so I didn't really have the confidence that I could achieve the goals and dreams I desired. Single mothers, supporting your children in what they desire to do as they are growing up is very important. A mother and father are the most influential people on earth in a childs life. If momma says it, or daddy says it, the child believes it—nobody else words matter, until they become teenagers....lol anyway. We have the greatest influence on our children. We make them who they are in the future. We need to encourage them in every positive thing they do, tell them they can do it no matter what, let them know that they are great, that they will get better as they keep practicing, and let them know there is nothing to fear. Then we can stand back and watch them become courageous individuals.

I know it's hard sometimes to focus on our children's futures, because we are so busy taking care of their day-to-day needs, however, it is important to remember we are leading and guiding them into the future, and when they get there, they need to have a sense of direction of what they are to do. I don't care if they change their career choice fifty times. Just change with them. At the same time, pray that God will give them clarity and show them clearly what they are here on earth to do. Also, be sure to support all your children. Don't favor one over the other. Do a self examination and make sure you're not leaning toward one more than another. If you are having a hard time getting along with a particular child, ask God and yourself why. Children can sense when their parent is showing favoritism toward another child, whether you believe you are or not.

I have a daughter that has very similar traits to me in every way. When she was younger, I had a difficult time with her behavior. She was challenging, busy, and just determined to do her own thing. Well, that went against the grain of what I wanted her to do, so I struggled with her a lot mainly because I was a control freak and I wanted her to do it my way instead of relaxing letting her grow and do it her way so long as it was not hurting her or anyone else. Then when she was about four years old, I remember hearing the Lord say to me within my heart, "Do you remember how you used to act when you were little?" I answered, "Yes." He said, "Well, she's very much like you, and many rejected you and wanted you to sit down, or be quiet, when all you were doing was being yourself. You did not like how they treated you, did you?" I said "No." He said, "Just treat her the way you would have wanted them to treat you and love her just for who she is. All she wants is your love." After that I remember taking her into my arms one day after disciplining her with a raging anger and just hugging her. That day she let out a sigh of relief, as if to say "Mom, I've been waiting for you to just hug me and love me for me." From that day I promised to love her just for whom she is, and I will for the rest of my life.

Also, I remember the day when I realized I struggled with negative feelings toward my son. I recognized I had not grown up with brothers, I had been abandoned by the most important men in my life, and most of my experiences with men throughout my life had been detrimental. I had not understood the behaviors of boys very much when I was young, and my mom was always trying to discourage me from being in contact with them, so that did not help my relationship with my son very much. I did not totally understand him, but I decided that I needed to accept him for who he was. I have a friend whose mother died when she was young, so she was raised by her father and also had six brothers. She understood men and was used to their different behaviors. I was glad God placed her in my life. I began talking to her about my son, and she would help me understand that many of the things my son was doing were normal, because her brothers had done many of the same types of things. Talking with her helped me relax and let my son be a boy. Single mothers, please don't deprive your sons or daughters of healthy, monitored relationships with the opposite sex. When you try to keep them separated, they don't learn how to interact with the opposite sex properly, and they end up doing foolish things, especially if they grow up without a father or mother around.

During my senior year in high school, I got pregnant and had my first abortion. My mother always told my sister and I, "All I want you all to do is just graduate from high school, and don't have any babies before you do. Do that and I'll be happy." Well, that was not enough, she should have set higher standards than that for us. We have to paint a bigger picture than that for our children. We have to dream big with them. We have to be sure to let them know that there is life beyond high school and more accomplishments that you are expecting them to reach. Getting pregnant is not the only accomplishment for a woman in life.

Well, when I found out that I was pregnant, I surely did not want to disappoint my mom, so I had an abortion. After all, they were teaching us back then that it was just a blood clot, not a formed baby yet until after so many weeks, and society made abortion seem easy and like it was the right thing to do. But, that teaching is a lie. As soon as you are pregnant, you are pregnant with a baby with a life, hope, and a future; however, I did not discover that truth until two abortions later.

I have three children, but I should have seven. I've only been preganant six times and one of those pregnancies were with twins. I'll never for get my very last abortion, I struggled tremendously with making the decision to get that abortion. I arrived at the abortion clinic on time but did not start the process until three hours later. When I got there I checked in and thought I was sure about this decision, until I realized I wasn't. The medical assistant acted as if she cared and she really wanted me to take my time and make the right decision. She suggested that I go through a second discussion session before beginning, so I did. After that was over I still couldn't do it, I asked if I could use the phone first. I wanted to call the father and make sure he really was sure that he did not want the baby. I could not reach him for a whole hour but I waited. Finally he answered and I asked him one last time if he was sure I should do this, hoping he would say no, but he didn't. Why did I give that much power over my life to another human being? I hung up the phone and continued the process. The medical assistant who peformed the abortion acted as if she was concerned and knew that this was a difficult decision for me, but that was just the devil in dequise. I knew that because after the abortion was complete she had enough courage to come into the recovery room and tell me, "I just wanted to let you know there were twins in there". What was I to do at that point? We sure couldn't bring them back! Later that night I went to the fathers house and I remember sitting on the couch, feeling lost and lifeless, we were watching television and all of a sudden I heard baby rattles and a baby crying, then it stopped. I turned to him and said angrily "who's baby is upstairs"? He looked at me and laughed and replied "nobody, what is the matter with you?, you crazy"? From that point on I knew I would never get another abortion another day in my life. I later gave birth two more times and I am still very fertile…. lol! You may be in a similar situation. Maybe you're facing a decision of whether to have a baby or an abortion. Let me tell you—have the baby and stop having sex until you get married. Don't get an abortion, because you never know who you're carrying in your body. You may be carrying the next president of the United States. Your mother gave you a chance, so give your baby a chance too. Besides—I kid you not—it seemed like every time I would get an abortion, I would get pregnant again. I started saying, "Man, for every abortion I have, I get another child anyway, so I may as well have them and shut my legs!" What I learned was if I don't want children, then I shouldn't have sex, because obviously I have been chosen on this earth to give birth to babies.

I graduated from high school in June of 1992, and after that first pregnancy and abortion during my senior year, by August I was pregnant a second time. Promiscuous little thing, wasn't I? It seemed like I couldn't get enough SEX, and it was easy to lay with a man who I really thought liked me. I had been introduced to sex at a very young age by all the infiltrating molesters that passed through my life. I learned how to do much at a very young age, so by the time I was in high school, I knew what I was doing and the ironic thing was I enjoyed it. How do you tell somebody that something that feels good is really bad for them—not easy to do, huh? I was caught up in masturbation at the age of 5, watching pornography videos at the age of 8 or 9, and I had my first phone sex experience in my teenage years. We are talking about a sexually involved and proficient young woman at this point.

If you have been molested early in your life, you may tend to like sex and to be very sexually active; or maybe you're the opposite—you like sex, but not really, because of the fact that your first sexual experience happened in the wrong way. I want to tell you that Jesus forgives and heals. I dealt with all of the molesters in my life by naming them one by one and forgiving each one of them as I asked God to forgive me for my sexual behaviors that resulted from their molestations. I also asked God to deliver me from the unrighteous sexual desires that I had acquired over the years and asked him to heal me of what they had done to me. Now don't get me wrong I still have sexual desires, but I know I have to wait to have sex until i'm married and when it gets to tough for me I have to call on Jesus for HELP! I forgave all them who hurt me sexually and God forgave me for carrying on with sexual immorality. He healed me of my past and now I can talk about it to help others. Just know one thing—it was not your fault. The one who molested you is the one who got you started, but Jesus and you are the one who can end this cycle of sexual immorality in your life.

When I found out I was pregnant again, I remember going to my mom feeling like it was okay that I was pregnant now, because after all, she did say no babies before I graduated, right? I told her I was pregnant, and she was still not pleased. I knew she was against abortions. I never really knew why, but I remember hearing her saying, "No, I don't believe in that," and that was pretty much all she said about the topic.

She taught me as much as she could, but what she failed to do was teach me the truth about sex. Sex outside of marriage is a sin and not pleasing in the sight of God. If you don't teach your children this, you will be setting them up for possible pregnancies outside of marriage, sexually transmitted diseases, prostitution and possibly death.

Single mothers, let's help our daughters not become single mothers like we have become. Teach them that their bodies are precious. Teach your children that they are princesses, queens, princes and kings. They need to wait for the right man/woman (Tell them God has some one He is preparing for them) to come along and treat them with dignity, honor and respect; someone who will recognize the value within them, and marry them. When commitment through marriage takes place that's when sexual intercourse has the right to take place.

Tell them they don't want to be spoiled goods and all used up before they connect with their spouse. Be real with them about the dangers of having sex outside of marriage. Teach them what God says about them and their bodies:

1 Corinthians 6:19

Do you not know that your **body** is the **temple** (the very sanctuary) of the Holy Spirit Who lives within you, whom you have received [as a Gift] from **God**? You are not your own.

Hebrews 13:4

Let marriage be had in honor among all, and let the bed be undefiled: for **fornicator**s and adulterers God will judge.

Revelation 21:8

But for the fearful, and unbelieving, and abominable, and murderers, and **fornicator**s, and sorcerers, and idolaters, and all liars, their part shall be in the lake that burns with fire and brimstone; which is the second death.

If only I had known all that—if only I had been preached to about it over and over throughout my life. We should also warn our children about molesters. Maybe then I would not have been so easily persuaded by the molesters in my life and the enemy that prompts them to molest. Also don't leave your helpless babies, toddlers, and school age children with people so easily. You shouldn't trust anybody with your precious children—not your neighbor, relative, nor stranger. It's just not safe. You may be saying, "But who's going to watch my children?"

First of all, God knows you need a sitter, so pray and ask God to provide you and your children with a safe and loving babysitter who will not harm your children or put them in harm's way. Then look at yourself and make right choices about where you go and when you go. Ask yourself and God whether or not you should take the children this time. Sometimes you may not need to go when you want to, because if your children are not in the right place at the right time, it could be a life changing experience and affect them for the rest of their lives.

I used to wonder if my mom did these things for me, because if she had, I would not have been infiltrated so much. But how could she preach, "Don't have sex until your married," to me when at times she was wrapped up in sex without marriage herself. When you open sexual doors in your life outside of marriage for yourself, then you open the same doors in your children's lives no matter what age they are. The sexual infiltrations may not come the same way you're indulging in them, but they will come in some form or another. My mother had boyfriends. At some points she had husbands, but she still slept with them before they were married. Now let me say she wasn't "out there"sleeping with any and everybody or anything like that, that I knew of, but she couldn't really convince me that sex without being married was a sin and not right if she was doing it, now could she? So maybe that's why she never tried to.

Mothers, let me tell you this—you have to set high standards for yourself if you want your children to have high standards for themselves. What you model in front of them is ultimately what they will think they can do. So if you want a child that's not all used up, than don't you become used up yourself. Keep yourself from the sin of fornication. Don't think you can go off and have secret rendezvous either, because God and the devil will see you and what you sow your child will reap.

It's sad that our children have to reap what we sow, but unfortunately they do. It's the law of reciprocity. That is what happens until either we break our bad habits, turn to Jesus and ask God to forgive us, or the children become old enough to understand what we have done and break those generational habits off in their own lives through the power of Jesus Christ and his righteousness—by doing the opposite of what we did.

chapter

THREE

Who is Faye? Continues.

Single mothers on the M.O.V.E. help steer their children in the right direction. They help their children reach for their dreams and goals. Tell your children they can. Tell them it's possible. Affirm their ideas—and take necessary steps to help them realize their dreams and goals. Don't just expect them to carry out their dreams without your help and direction, or they will make more mistakes than necessary, don't get me wrong there are some children out there who just some how seem to know what they want, but most children need parental guidance and some children don't want to listen at all.

I had my first baby boy in 1993. My mother was wonderful, even though it did not make her happy to hear that I was pregnant. She still loved her grandson and I. She purchased everything we needed. I worked real hard before he was born and accomplished moving into my first apartment, but she furnished it. She was a great financial support (notice ladies I haven't said anything about the daddy helping, because he did not this is why you need to choose the father of your children carefully). My mother has always been a great financial support. My dream is to help support her one day.

With all that I had, I still found myself alone in that apartment raising my son. During the first three days of being home from the hospital after giving birth to my son, I needed some money to pay the bills. So, I decided to connect with people who could help me (at least at the time I thought they were my help). I was able to get some cocaine given to me on credit. I had tried doing this sort of thing prior to becoming pregnant, but it did not workout each time I tried I always took a lost so, I stopped after being caught in a drug raid when I was 17 years old.

Well this time after going back into the drug game, I was set up by some people. They set me up with undercover cops, because they had been caught and needed a scapegoat to get them out of trouble (sort of like Jesus, He was our scapegoat to get us out of trouble for our sins), and they chose me. The customers/undercover cops came to my house the first time to buy drugs when my son was just three days old. I went to them the second time about three weeks later. The third time they tried to get me to sell to them, I refused, because I did not need anymore money.

I'm telling you, when I look back, it had to be the protection of God that kept them from arresting me right on the spot the first time. I sold drugs to them in my house. They could have taken me and my baby, and I would have lost everything instantly. God's protection was around me even when I didn't know it or want Him. When you don't have Jesus in your life, you'll do anything. Bishop T.D. Jakes quoted, "Desperate people do desperate things," and I happened to be one of those desperate people at that point in my life.

I wasn't actually arrested until one year later when I was pulled over by the police and they discovered there was a warrant out for my arrest. I couldn't think of anything I had done, but, oh, how soon we forget the dirt we do, especially when we don't care about anybody but ourselves. When I arrived at the police station and they informed me of the reason the warrant was issued, I couldn't believe it. I was stunned to find out I had been set up.

At this point, my son was almost a one year old, and all I could think about was who would raise him? That night I sat in that jail cell still without Christ in my life, and when I tell you my mind was over-loaded with thoughts, it was. I mean, I had never in my life had so many thoughts racing through my mind so fast at once. Now I understand what people with mental problems go through. I felt like I had a bunch of invisible people standing around me in that cell interrogating me with questions of worry, one after another. It was only by the Grace of God I did not have a nervous breakdown and get escorted to the mental ward that night. I could not stop the thoughts from flowing through my head. All I remember was laying my head down, closing my eyes, and saying to myself, "If I just close my eyes and go to sleep, these thoughts will go away," and that's what I did.

Somewhere between the night I was arrested and my sentencing date, I received Jesus in my heart as my personal savior, and I believe this was God's way of proving to me he was real and in control of my life. I had always gone to church, because my mom raised us up to go to church, but I never really knew Jesus. Nevertheless, one day, watching television as Pat Robertson of the 700 Club began to share the Gospel of Jesus Christ through the airwaves, something inside of me said, "That's what you need. Pray with him." I prayed the sinner's prayer, and from that moment, my life began to change.

I still had to go through the trial with the courts, but I remembered hearing the old folks say all the time when I was young that, "The truth will set you free," so I began to stand on that word, even though I had never read it. I said, "God, they said, that you said, "the truth will set me free", so I'm just going to tell the truth about everything, and I believe you will get me out of this." From that point on, every time I had to see a judge, probation officer, or counselor, I told them the absolute truth about anything they asked me. Even through all that, they still recommended ten to twenty years in prison. You know what? I still kept reminding myself, "The truth will set me free."

As I went through this long, dragged out case I can say I found out that prayer works. Every prayer I prayed through the whole process I saw God answer it. One year later it was suggested by the pre-probation officer to the judge that I receive ten to twenty years for each count, I had two counts. The night before being sentenced, I said a prayer that went sort of like this, "God please help me tomorrow when I stand in front of the judge for sentencing. Let the judge get a good night sleep and feel good and refreshed when he judges my case. Let him make the right decision about me."

Before I stood up in front of the judge, I sat in that courtroom holding my son with tears streaming down my face, not knowing what would happen to me. But when I finally stood up to receive my sentence that really only God could give me, the judge let out a yawn as he covered his mouth and said, "Hmmm, I feel kind of good this morning, I must have gotten a good night sleep last night." I was blown away at what I had just witnessed with my own ears and eyes. I had seen God answer my prayer and that amazed me. It was during this time when I finally became convinced that prayer really does work.

When my name was called to approach the bench, I stood there and said all that I had to say to the judge. I let him know I was a college student with two jobs and that I had received Jesus in my heart as my personal savior. The judge looked at me and said, "I'm going to give you a nine month waiting period before sentencing you for this crime, to prove to me that you have really turned your life around, and if you make it through the nine months without trouble, I'll only give you two years probation. If you fail, I'm giving you prison time."

I was happy, but sad, because I felt like I was now under a microscope and I had to do right, because if I messed up, it would be over for me. Well, let me tell you, I did mess up. During that waiting period I was ordered to report to a probation officer and do weekly drug screening drops, and although I had received Jesus, I had not completely turned away from certain sins yet, so I was still clubbing, sexing, and doing drugs. I am a living witness that God delivers, even if it is a process of time. Once I understood that certain things I did were sins and not pleasing to God I would immediately begin praying to God for help in stopping these sins until I stopped.

During the waiting period I had dirty drops and I had to go before the judge twice. Each time I would just say, "Judge, I'm addicted to marijuana, and I try not to smoke, but when things get stressful for me I have smoked it." Again I was truthful with him. He looked at me and said, "Well, I'm going to have to give you two weekends in jail."

Still God caused him to be merciful to me. He could have said, "You're done! Go to prison. You were here for drugs, and now you're doing drugs. Just go to prison." He didn't, however, because God wouldn't let him. It took me one year of constant prayer to God saying, "Lord please help me not to smoke anymore." Every time I would smoke a blunt I would go home and say, "God help me, why do I continue to do this? I don't want to smoke. What do I have to do to quit?" When I asked God that question I heard him say, "First thing you're going to have to do is stop going around the people who are smoking." Well—that was an eye opener. I asked for a way out, but I did not know it would cause me to release my friends. At that point I had a choice to either be free or stay bound. It wasn't easy, but I chose to let the people go. It was to the point where when I was around them that I wasn't comfortable anymore, so why did I keep going and hanging out with them anyway?

When I made that choice, after that day, I stopped smoking marijuana completely. I don't even know when it was exactly—all I know is that I stopped. When we are asking God for something, he will always ask us for something in return, and we have to be willing to give it to him if we really want to be free. It doesn't matter what it is. So, God, through the judge, gave me another chance—right? And he did not send me to prison because of those dirty drops.

Mothers, nobody controls our destiny but God. I want all you *Single Mothers on the M.O.V.E.*, to know that the Bible says, "The heart of the king (the one who's in charge) is in the hand of God," and God can turn it any way he wants to concerning our lives. Truly God has proven that to me. When it was all said and done, and I went back to the courts after the nine month waiting period to get sentenced, the judge gave me two years' probation with weekly drug screenings for one year.

God is good. He spared my life and my son's life too. When my son turned ten years old, I was so grateful to be able to be with him, all I could say is, thank you Jesus.

God is still perfecting me

I haven't arrived, but, oh my God, I'm truly not where I used to be. Single Mothers, He can do the same for you if you only believe. Ask Him to come into your life, come into your heart, and save you from the sins that you are committing right now. Tell Him you're sorry and that you want to turn away from the sins. Command evil to leave you and ask God to help you. Ask him to wash away the sins you have commited with the blood of Jesus that was shed on the cross in exchange for your sins. He died for you and me so that we can be free from sin. If you just prayed and ask God to do that for you log into my guestbook and let me know at www.lashandafaye.info. There were many other sins I was wrapped up in and thanks be to God he set me free from them and he can do the same for you. Whatever it is, you can go to him with it. Whether it's prostitution (paid or unpaid), pornography (television, books, or computer), phone sex (masturbation), gambling (daily3/4, scratch offs, or casinos), lying (small or big), fornication (sex without being married), cheating (holding back information), scheming to get what you need or want (slick talking and manipulation), drugs (illegal or prescribed), or thievery.

You name it, I've done it, all of it, but I'm free from it because "Whom the Son (Jesus) makes free is free indeed." Does the temptation to commit those sins come back to tempt me? Yes, it does. Have I fallen into some of them after receiving Jesus? Yes, I have. But did I continue with them? No, I did not. What I did was go to someone I could trust and I told them about the struggle I was in and that I did not want to be in it. I asked them to pray with me. They prayed with me and gave me instructions on how to overcome these sins and remain free of them. I got up and kept on moving forward in God and now when I struggle I go to God in Jesus name and power, because it's through Him are we set free. One thing the devil wants us to do is to give up, stop going to God, turn back around and go back to living the way we were before we made a choice to live for Christ. We can never let him win. We must continue to fight the good fight of faith, and live for God.

We don't have to sin. Jesus Christ took sin on the cross with Him when He died for us. We are free from sin and free to do the right thing. Just ask Him to help you.

I have shared who I was and who I am, but to sum it up, I am a blood-bought child of God, saved, delivered, and set free from the sinful nature of this world, and I can truly say I'm changed, never to be the same again. I will fulfill destiny and my purpose for as long as I'm on this earth—and you can too.

chapter

FOUR

What is a Single Mother on the M.O.V.E.?
"Are You One"?

A *Single Mother on the M.O.V.E.* is a woman who can't just sit still and watch life pass her by without reaching out to fulfill a certain purpose in life, for both herself and her children. She will take note of the natural gifts, talents and abilities inside her as well as her children, and once she recognizes them, she will take steps to develop them.

When she discovers her God-given gifts and talents, oppression can't suppress her and depression can't hold her down. Doubt may come, but she'll still move forward. She'll do it afraid and unsure, but she will do it. Thoughts of weariness will come, but there is something about a single mother on the move that keeps her going. What is it? It's the fact that she is on the **M.O.V.E.**

M—Stands for a *Single Mother on the M.O.V.E* Being Motivated

A *Single Mother on the M.O.V.E* is motivated to rise daily and carry out the necessary duties that will keep her life in order. Her children are what motivates her the most. She realizes that she has to pull it together and keep it together if for nobody else, the children. A single mother spends time praying and reading the bible daily in order for her day to go well; reading the bible daily does not come overnight but it's a continual persevering process. After including God in her daily life, she has a orderly structured daily life style, she stays on top of the laundry making sure food is prepared for the family daily—not just any food, but healthy meals. She's motivated to drop by her children's school to check on them, or she e-mails her children's teachers, keeping communication lines open between herself and the school as much as possible. This mother is also one who is motivated to assure her children become acquainted with responsibility, such as how to clean a home properly, teaching them things like how to do laundry and hang their clothing, how to budget and pay bills properly. This prepares them for future independence. A motivated mother makes sure she plans time to bond with her children to build strong love and unity in the house. She includes family prayer and Bible reading time with her children, because she knows she is responsible for making sure they know who God is. No one has to motivate her to go to work daily. She understands she is the breadwinner and makes no excuses for missing work, even if it hurts sometimes while she's there.

Motivation, to me, is an action word—you're always ready to move. When you are motivated, you are inspired to accomplish something, and when your life is progressing and improving in the direction of success and completion of things you have started, than you can say you're motivated. Motivated, according to dictionary.com, means to provide with an incentive; **move to action**; and/or impel.

What is your incentive for being motivated? Sometimes incentive for motivation could be explained with simple words like "it's just the right thing to do," or "if my house is clean I'll feel better"—not "if my house is clean I'll impress the man, I'll get the man, or I'll keep the man." Some of you ladies know what I'm talking about. I mean, I like to clean, but I remember when I would clean extra special if I knew someone was coming over. A truly motivated person cleans up special every time, just because she's motivated by the mere thought of "it's the right thing to do." We need to check ourselves when we are motivated and see what is motivating us, and just make sure we have pure motives with good intentions to follow them. Being motivated brings prosperity to our lives and is contagious to other people around us, which is a good thing. Be motivated for you and nobody else. If you can't be motivated for you, then you need to love you just a little bit more. Know that you are special and worth staying motivated for, just to make you and your children's lives better.

O—Stands for a *Single Mother on the M.O.V.E.* Being Ongoing

When you're ongoing, you never quit, regardless of how you feel. You may want to give up—as a matter of fact, you slack off a bit, but because there are dreams inside of you that want to live, you find yourself going right back to the thing you said, "Well forget it, it's just not for me." You go back and you pick up where you left off, because you can't give up. Why?—because you're ongoing. You know you're ongoing when you haven't seen someone for years, and when you see them, you are still talking about the same good values you talked about when you saw them years ago.

Take salvation, for instance. When I gave my life to Christ, I told my friends and they said okay, and when they saw me one year later, I was still telling them Jesus loves you. When I saw them three years later, I was still saying Jesus loves you. Ten years later, I see them—and, yes, I'm still saying Jesus loves you. I would say I'm pretty much in an ongoing mode in my relationship with Christ. I may have had some bad days, but I have remained in my relationship with my Savior. Ongoing, according to dictionary.com, means continuing without termination or interruption. I agree with that definition, except for the interruption part, because I have had interruptions in my life that have caused me to lose my focus a bit, but I knew that if I didn't finish what I had started, then I wouldn't be satisfied with me, so I got back to what I knew I should be doing.

V—Stands for a *Single Mother on the M.O.V.E.* Being Victorious

When a *Single Mother on the M.O.V.E.* is victorious, she has overcome all her struggles, immoral ways, and challenges of every kind. Everything she endeavors to do she achieves, even if it does take a little more time than expected. Victorious, according to dictionary.com, means having achieved a victory; conquering; and/or triumphant. Not only does a *Single Mother on the M.O.V.E.* go through life conquering, but I believe she is "more than a conqueror." In Romans 8:37, the scripture says, "No, in all these things we are more than conquerors through Him who loved us." Who loves you? Jesus loves you.

You can conquer any challenge that comes your way by asking God for help. Did you hear that "No" at the beginning of the scripture? That is saying no to the mountains, people, or troubles that try to get in your way and stop you. You have to say, "No, I'm not going to be defeated by anything that tries to hold me back from being more than a conqueror over…" this drug habit, these college courses, this break-up between me and the wrong man for me. I can get the victory over this situation. I can lose this weight and move in the right direction. To me "…more than a conqueror…" means that I am a ruler, and when you are a ruler you control what's trying to get the best of you and you get the best of it—you determine whether you win or lose. Will the negative rise above the positive and overtake your life or will you take the negative down by its neck and rule with the positive? You determine the outcome by how you think and the actions you take toward a situation. Say this with me, "I will have victory, because I will rule over every negative situation that comes into my life."

E—Stands for a *Single Mother on the M.O.V.E.* Being Encouraged

Single Mothers, being encouraged means you continue to see the good in a situation, even during times when it looks like the bad outweighs the good. That's when you have to step outside of yourself and find someone you can trust to help you look for the good in order to stay encouraged. And when you're encouraged, you can encourage other people. Encouraged, according to dictionary.com, means to promote, advance, or foster.

How do I stay encouraged? I believe it is important to promote good habits in your life, like eating healthy, exercising, and taking vitamins. This will help you feel good physically, so that you feel encouraged emotionally. Always find ways to advance yourself to the next level of success in your life. If you think you have done all you can do, learned all you can learn, you're wrong. Look for a new recipe to try, a new subject to learn about that interests you, a new newspaper article to read—something that will keep you advancing mentally in life.

While you're advancing, remember to foster something or someone. Foster simply means to care for or cherish. The Bible tells me that a man named David encouraged himself in the Lord, which means I have to encourage myself in the Lord. Many times, therefore, I sing songs to Jesus, I read the Bible, and I pray throughout the day, and by doing so, I'm fostering my relationship with God. I also read other clean, uplifting materials that motivate me, which helps me make positive changes in my life. I go to church, I fellowship with positive people who speak encouraging words to me, and I make sure when I get negative thoughts in my mind, I disagree with them by simply saying, "No, I don't receive that thought for my life, I do not agree with that, and I will not do that, in Jesus' name;" or "That will not happen, this is what I'm going to do;" or "This is what is going to happen." By doing this, I stay victorious. Then I begin to pray, asking God to help me in the weak areas of my life, so that I can continue to stay encouraged and keep going in the right direction. Not only should you continue to promote, advance, and foster yourself, but you should actively do the same for your children, as well as others.

If you fit the descriptions above, then congratulations! You are a *Single Mother on the M.O.V.E.* If you are not yet all these things, you can become them slowly but surely, because all things are possible if you believe. Just believe you can, put some action behind your believing, and you'll be on your way to becoming a *Single Mother on the M.O.V.E.*

chapter

FIVE

Be Wise in Your Thoughts

A *Single Mother on the M.O.V.E.* has no time to think negative thoughts, because she has discovered that negative thought produce negative actions. We must speak and pray against negative thoughts; combat them with positive words. Prayer is a single mother's strategy to get from one place to the next in her life.

Proverbs 4:7 says, "Wisdom is the principal thing; therefore get wisdom: and with all you're getting, get **understanding**."

A *Single Mother on the M.O.V.E.* understands that her responsibility is so big that she cannot possibly handle it all by herself. She needs the Lord. She needs positive people around her; mentors who are not afraid, intimidated, or jealous of her; mentors who will be bold enough to tell her the good, bad, and ugly about herself; mentors who will give her counsel on how to overcome her dilemmas, so that she can move forward into her promised destiny, dreams, visions, and successes that are not only for her, but for her children and others who she will cross paths with as she moves forward.

It takes humility, to be able to say "I don't know it all, so I'd better ask somebody else who I believe will have answers, before I screw up."

Throughout life, single mothers worry about many things. We ask ourselves, "What will we eat? How will I buy the children's necessities for school? How will I pay the bills?" One thing I've found out is, "**I**" don't have to do a thing. The Lord spoke to me long ago in an audible voice and told me "Don't worry." He said, "When you begin to worry, I want you to ask yourself a few questions." These are the questions he said to ask myself:

Can I fix the situation? If the answer is no, "Don't worry."

Can I change what is done? If the answer is no, "Don't worry."

Do I have what I need or any way of getting what I need within my own power—without God? If the answer is no, "Don't worry."

My answer to all those questions in the situations I was facing was, "No." There was nothing I could do about them, so he said "Then don't worry." Little did I know he was teaching me how to trust Him, and, sure enough, the problems would always be taken care of. I didn't know how, but somehow what I needed would always be supplied. So I learned how to wait, and as I waited, my patience and trust in God grew.

Single Mothers, we may have thoughts of failure or regret, such as, "If I had not had these children before I was ready, I would be a better parent. I made wrong choices in my life. I'm a failure, and that's why I'm living this way."

Doubts may arise like, "Nothing will ever change in my life. I'll never be able to give my children the best. We're always going to live in poverty."

All those thoughts may be floating around in your mind. You know what they are telling you? "YOU CAN'T!" and "LIFE IS NOT GOING TO GET BETTER FOR YOU!"

But you know what? I'm here to challenge you, right in the face of doubt, failure, and regret, and say to you, "YOU CAN! THIS TOO SHALL PASS."

You've got to know that all of what you're going through is just to make you stronger for what you have got to face in the future. These trials are helping you to grow up so you can be ready to handle some great opportunities in your future. You won't always be a single mother. The kids will grow up, and you will look back and say, "I made it." The thoughts that go through your mind making you believe your situation can't possibly change are hopeless thoughts. But your situation can change.

I'm reminded of a mother who bought the lies of the enemy speaking to her, and she gave in and left her children. She could not resist her hopeless thoughts, but if she had just held on a little bit longer, God would have worked it out for her. How do I know? Because I get the same thoughts, but when I do, I firmly make powerful, positive statements to myself, and the hopelessness dissipates. I know to whom I belong, and as long as I have King Jesus, all things will work out in my life for good.

Now—you begin to speak to the thoughts in your mind, and say the opposite of what they are saying to you. Talk back to the thoughts! If you were in a confrontation with a physical person, and that person was telling you something that you didn't like, you would defend yourself, right? Do the same to the hopeless, negative thoughts that are coming into your mind. Talk back to them and tell them the reverse of what they are telling you. Then add in what you want to happen in your life and your children's lives, too.

If your thoughts say, "That's impossible; I can never do that," then you say, "You're a lying thought, and I'm not going to accept what you're saying to me. I can do anything I want to, if I put my mind to it. If I take action, persevere, and never give up until I see it happen, I can do it." Furthermore I can do it because the Bible says, "I can do all things through Christ Jesus who gives me the strength to do it." Say that and that will really shut up those devilish thoughts!

This is how you combat negative thoughts. You have to be determined, stay diligent about it, and be on guard against these thoughts when they come. Catch them, throw them down, and speak against them. As you do this, you will continue to move forward toward the goals you have set for yourself.

Recap:

1. A *Single Mother on the M.O.V.E.* is:

M—motivated

O—ongoing

V—victorious

E—encouraged

2. She prays continuously.

3. She seeks out understanding in any given situation, which means she understands she can't handle the single mother journey on her own.

4. She remembers not to worry.

chapter

SIX

Single Momma, Are You Steeped in Debt?

You may be in over your head with debt. So was I, but we cannot allow our circumstances to stop us and get us down. We must fight our way to financial stability by being disciplined in our spending habits and giving. We have to get to the point where we say, "No, girl you are not having that today." Ask yourself these two questions before buying something: Do I have a real, true, genuine need for this right now in my life, or do I just want it?

Wants and needs are two different things. In America we get what we want more than we get what we need. People in many other countries don't even understand what getting what they want means. They are just thankful for getting what they need.

Once you ask yourself, before purchasing something, "Do I need this, or want this," and answer truthfully, your answer will be your way of escape from spending unnecessary money. If your answer is a legitimate yes, then go ahead and purchase what you need. That's fine, but another thing you can ask yourself is, "Can I wait another two weeks for this and pay a bill with this instead, or do I really need this right this moment?" If you're really honest with yourself, you might even be able to wait until after you get your next two pay checks, because maybe you're not even taking that trip you 've planned for another two months, or you haven't even run out of that certain product you use. Some of us just like the way it feels to shop, pick items out, and spend money.

You see, real money spenders, shoppers, or whatever you want to call us, forget about tomorrow. We just shop for today (I'm talking about the real money spenders), and we have to end that in our lives. We have to become more responsible. This means holding on to our money and waiting for the right opportunities to spend it, not when we want to or when we think we should, but when it is the right time. When we really get a hold of our spending habits, we'll be blessed with more, because God will see that He can trust us with what He has already given us. We'll still get that fulfillment that we get when we spend money, however, we'll get better deals, because God will reward our discipline of waiting and saving.

Let the Money Sit in the Bank

Let's talk about money that has no direction, the left over money that you don't know what to do with—after you have paid all the bills, you have all the clothing, shoes and groceries you need, and you just don't need anything else. That's the money I'm talking about. It may be $5 for some, or $50 or $500 for others. I suggest you let that money sit in the bank and wait to use it for what is necessary. This was the hardest thing for me to do, but I conquered it. I can't even begin to tell you how God then began to increase and add to my finances, because He saw that I no longer wanted to be a money waster. He saw that I wanted to be a money saver for his purposes, which are the right purposes. I was the type of person who had to spend money daily. It seemed like I could always find a reason to spend some money. To this day I fight against that.

I have also found out something about the smaller amount of money that seems to have no purpose. Usually you're going to spend it before the week is over on—hmmmm, "Nothing, really." Well that money does have a purpose. It has a purpose somewhere in this world, in some community somewhere. When I don't know what to do with extra money, I give it away to a church, or nonprofit organization of some sort. After all, I am a spender, so I spend money investing in others, because I know I'll be rewarded later for giving to needy people, missions, or wherever my heart says to give money. It hurts sometimes, but I made a commitment to do so. I wanted to see what the results of giving to individuals or organizational outreaches would be, versus the results of giving to Subway, Burger King, or the mall, just for me.

The results have been phenomenal. I am now more disciplined than ever before. I always have what I need, and I also get blessed with what I want at below normal prices. I'm also almost at a place of debt freedom. I am able to pay my bills when they are due without struggle. Previously, I couldn't even look at my bills.

I have received free vacations, I was blessed to drive a brand new 2007 vehicle, which I wasn't expecting to get, so my first brand new 1994 vehicle that I lost to the gambling addiction I had was replaced all because of my choice to discipline my spending habits. I have learned that material things come and go and what I drive is not what is most important. I believe these blessing from God are a result of my giving to people and places that He tells me to. I could go on with countless things my children and I have received, but it would take too much paper and ink to tell you.(LoL)!

God has blessed me to discipline myself and pay cash for what I get instead of credit as I have in the past. My goal is to never use credit another day in my life. I want to pay for everything with cash, check, or money order and my moto is "i get the best for less". My children and I never lack what is needed.

Listen, Single Mothers, we have bills to pay, debts to pay, and children to be concerned about, so we have to use our money wisely even when we get married. We have to continue using our same budgeting habits. We can't get so excited and begin thinking, "Well, I'm married now, so I'm going to have extra money to spend because my husband will be paying the bills."

No, that's not right. He will need you to remain disciplined with your money. So, please don't get too happy.

You may be in debt right now as you are reading this book, and what I would say to you is what a very wise man said to me one day. He said, "Get back to the basics," the basics that you were taught in kindergarten, first, second, and third grade—simple adding and subtracting. Go to an office supply store, get a personal ledger budget book, and begin to track your bills and spending habits. Develop a budget, and if something is not in your budget, don't spend money for it, unless, as I said before, it is an absolute necessity.

Single Mothers, we may have to sacrifice a little when attempting to come out of debt. Maybe you can select a more affordable hair dresser with reasonable prices or just get your hair done once a month instead of once a week. You may have to buy groceries and eat at home instead of eating out all the time. Temporarily stop the pedicures, manicures and false nails, and use the extra money to pay off your debt.

If you have the self control, and you can let money sit in the bank until you get enough to pay certain debts in full, do that, if not, pay as you go. If you're not making enough money to pay debts at all, but you have an extra $5 here and there you could use that to pay on the debt. If you would rather wait as some do then I say give it to a needy organization, and as you give those $5 or $10 to the poor and needy. God will then increase your finances and you will be able to eliminate your debts. You will see an increase in your finances, a drastic increase where you were not getting enough money.

Once all your debts are paid, begin to build a savings account with the leftover money. Again, before you use it, make sure it is for an emergency or something you actually need. Look at it, otherwise, as a giving account (money to give to help others). Don't worry about your vacations and money for other non-necessities. God will bless you with that. Strategize with a monthly budget and you will see the provision for what you desire. All things will work together for your good, because you are doing things the wise way (which is God's way—the right way).

chapter

SEVEN

What's the Matter with Higher Learning?

Not only was I in debt, but I didn't have a college degree. Studies show that people with college degrees make $20,000 more per year than people without college degrees. What I did as a single mother 32 years old was decide to hide behind the college life. Come hell or high water, I was going to get my bachelors degree. I got the financial aid, loans, scholarships, work study, state welfare assistance, you name it. I was going to take advantage of it all until I finished my degree and got a good job. It wasn't as easy, however, as I thought it would be. Here I was a single mother of three with no real support, I was crying through every math class I had, and I'm still working on getting the degree today. I began to ask myself if this was really necessary.

Yes, having a college degree does open doors in the job market that maybe wouldn't be opened for you otherwise. Remember, however, who I am—a Single Mother on the M.O.V.E. I am Motivated, Ongoing, Victorious, and Encouraged, we tend to make things happen, so you know I couldn't wait on the college degree.

During my first semester in college, I took my first English class, and I saw something come out of me that I had never really paid attention to before. I saw my intense desire to write, and the way I felt when I wrote was very releasing. I realized that I could get points across better when I wrote, so I thought—maybe I could be a writer. I had written poems, songs, books, and plays in the past, but I never saw myself as a true writer—certainly not a real author.

Through that English class, the gift that God placed in my life from the beginning began to illuminate inside of me and pour out of me onto paper. I remember asking my proffessor if she thought I was a good enough writer to be an author and her reply was, yes. I don't know if she was just being nice or what….lol, but I took that yes and ran with it. Wow, I thought, this is awesome! I'm an author! That is what higher education can do for you. It can cause you to see gifts, talents, and abilities that have been in you since birth, but have not come alive or been revealed yet. As I discovered the gift of writing within me, I began to take action. That's what a Single Mother on the M.O.V.E. does.

I began to ask God how I could fulfill my calling as a writer and make a career out of it. I wanted to enjoy writing, while reaching out to people who needed help and encouragement. This is what you have to do when you recognize your gift or talent that comes naturally and you have a passion for it. Ask God to show you the way to develop and use it successfully for both His purposes and yours.

So, the bottom line is, if you have finished high school, go to college. Going to college can't hurt you. It will only help you, even if it does take five or ten years to earn a degree. You are going to find out other things of value about yourself along the way.

Don't put off your education any longer than you have to. You may find out the very thing you were called to do on earth, sometimes through just one class. I did!

chapter

EIGHT

Love or Lust; Which Is It?

Remember in grade school when you liked your first boy, and all you wanted to do was maybe hold his jacket while he played football with the other boys, or give him some of your lunch? Maybe you even wanted to kiss him. Oh, how we go through many different emotions when we like a boy.

I remember when I first realized what love really was. There was this guy I was deeply in lust with. I liked this guy so much that he could do just about anything to me. He could cheat on me, forget my birthday, barely want to be seen in public with me, but, oh, I thought I loved him and he loved me. I took that man back at the drop of a hat more than once, because I thought he loved me. Then one day we broke up a final time—he did not want me anymore. That was a hard period in my life. Somehow around that time, I came across the scripture in the bible. First Corinthians, Chapter 13 that talks about love, and this it what it says:

⁴Love is patient, love is kind. It does not envy, it does not boast, it is not proud. ⁵It is not rude, it is not self-seeking, it is not easily angered, and it keeps no record of wrongs. ⁶Love does not delight in evil but rejoices with the truth. ⁷It always protects, always trusts, always hopes, and always perseveres.

⁸Love never fails.

New International Version

After reading that, I was absolutely convinced that man did not love me. Then every time I thought about getting back with him, wishing he would call me, or thinking I should call him, I would say over and over to myself, "He doesn't love me, he doesn't love me, he doesn't love me," because I had found out what true love really was, and he had not been showing any of that to me. Maybe he had a little bit in the beginning, but after a while that had ceased, and I needed to get out and stay out. With my new knowledge and determination, I was able to move forward from lust to real love.

Lust will have you running after a man. You will pursue him, call him, and stop everything for him. If you are doing all you can do to please him, and he's not acting right or doing the same in return, then you probably started the relationship based on lust and not wisdom.

A Single Mother on The M.O.V.E. does not go after men. She doesn't have time. She is one who is busy bringing definition to who she and her children are on earth. She is focused on recognizing and understanding her value and also making sure her children understand their value in life. Her focus is on bringing order to her daily household duties, making sure her children are properly cared for, keeping them focused in school, and meeting their emotional needs as well as their physical and spiritual needs.

She is one that endeavors to understand her gifts and callings that God has placed within her, so that she can be effectively used on earth to touch someone else's life with her gifts and calling. She's busy seeking the face of God to fulfill the destiny for which He created her to fulfill. She understands she does not have the ability or strength all by herself to do everything, so she must take time to sit at the feet of Jesus. This means she spends quiet time alone to pray and to listen to what God has to say to her on a daily basis. God has specific instructions to give to her, and it is in His presence where she is able to get direction, rejuvenation and understanding to live another successful day of life on earth.

God's presence is with you every where, in that quiet room in which you choose to talk to Him, or at your desk reading your Bible, or on the floor lying flat on your stomach just waiting to be touched by His Spirit. You choose that special place to be with him. I promise you wherever you choose, he will meet you there.

We live in a natural world and face natural circumstances, so we have to be ready to take on those natural things, like children, finances, difficult co-workers, neighbors, or the men that come our way. I'm here to tell you that if you sit in the Father God's lap daily, or lie in his bed chambers through prayer, you will not need a man as much as you think you do. God can satisfy you.

I have met women who go from man to man because they don't want to be alone, or they think that having a man is having love. I was one of them. I found out, however, that just because you have a man, doesn't mean you automatically have love. God is Love. He loves you, and he's all you need until he decides to bless you, if he does, with a mate.

I lived many years of my life having sex—I'd slept with my share of men—until one day I looked around and realize I was yet alone and wondered, "Where were they?"

I had given them the thing that should have been most precious to me, my body, spirit and soul; because I thought it would be precious to them. Turned out it wasn't. How many more men did I have to sleep with before I realized there was a pattern going on? And this pattern was not working, because I was still very much by myself.

One day in November of 1998, I gave it all up. I decided I was not going to hell for a man, and from that point until now, I have not given my self to anyone. I want the man God has for me, and the only way I will get him is by allowing God to send him while waiting through a period of abstinence. It has not been easy, but I give God all the credit for keeping me from falling into the bed of fornication again. I don't trust my judgment anymore, because I sit here three children later and still no husband, so i'll wait until I believe God shows me who the right guy is.

All my life I went after men. If I saw one, liked him, and wanted him, I could never wait to see whether he would notice me, like me, or want me. I wanted him, so I went after him. The problem was, I would go after men who were out of my reach in one way or another; whether they were of a different caliber than I was, to old for me as a minor, lived in a different city, or simply hadn't even noticed me. I made sure that eventually they knew there was a LaShanda, and when it was difficult to get him, I tried even harder until I got him.

I was talking to the Lord one day, reflecting on my past behaviors regarding men, and I said, "Why do I pursue men, especially men that I can't have ?"

As I began to meditate, thinking about why I was the way I was. I believe God began to show me how my biological father and other men who had played the role of a father in my life had rejected and abandoned me when I was younger. I had somewhat of a relationship with my stepfather as I was growing up. I actually thought he was my real father, until one day I was getting candy in a candy store at the age of seven, and an older lady behind the counter decided she would tell me that my father—at least the man who I had thought was my father—was really not my father. There I was, a seven year old little girl standing there getting one of my favorite things in my young life, candy, and this lady (who I later found out was my gradmother) tells me that an even more favorite and important thing to me, my dad, was not really my dad. That day was a turning point for the rest of my life. It pulled a measure of stability right out from underneath me.

Well, the good thing is that my stepfather never turned his back on me completely. He did try to somewhat participate in my life, and he continued paying child support for me my whole life. He gets a lot of credit for that, because where a person's money is, that is where their heart is also, so I know that he loved me. Anyway, I would always cry for him when he and my mom divorced.

"I want my daddy," I would say, but I could never have him the way I wanted him because he didn't live with us. He and my mom were separated and divorced when I was between three and five years old.

My mom and I moved to another city away from him, so I really missed him. I wanted him there daily to play with me, give me the attention that I needed, hug me, kiss me, tell me how beautiful I was, and just do what fathers should do.

I would see him every now and then, and when I did see him, he would show me love, but we always had to part from each other's company. Every time, when he left me, I would feel abandoned and hurt. I was abandoned by my real father and felt abandoned by my stepfather, so this is the picture of men that I had. If my stepfather would tell me he was coming to get me or going to fix my bike, and he didn't show up, that was a form of rejection, lying, and abandonment again. When I did finally see him, I was so happy to see him that I would just accept the rejection, the lying, and abandonment as normal and forget about it. It was simply part of what came along with having a dad. I would forget about the previous pain I had felt, how I had checked out the window to see if it was him every time a car went by, and when he didn't show up or call me for months at a time after saying he would, I would just be glad to see him when I did. How often are we just glad to be with the man when we can, even when we know he's been out all night with the other woman, or he did not make it over on a weekend, because he had to spend time with his wife and family?

So, as I meditated, what God was showing me about me is that I automatically thought that going after a man was normal and okay, even if he didn't respond to me, because that is what I had been introduced to as a newborn baby and child growing up. That's why I could blow up a man's pager, or leave 20 voicemails on his cell phone, or, better yet, sit outside his house when he did not make it home when he said he would, because I was programmed to go after a man either in a civil way—or a crazy way. What about if the man I wanted didn't want me, or did not notice me? Well, I just kept going after him until I got him one way or the other. Why was I so drawn to the ones who rejected or abandoned me? It reflected the interaction of what the very first men in my life—my "fathers"—had taught me? Yes, it was. I cried until they came, and when they did, I was happy, forgetting all the pain I had been through while waiting for them to come. Thus, pain wasn't really pain anymore; by the time I was old enough to want men, it was just normal.

Watching my mother as a role model, I also saw how she was left and done wrong by men, but what would she do? She would take them back again and again. Mothers, we have got to set high standards for our children. We can't necessarily control what their fathers do, but we can change what we allow men to do to us in front of them. We can speak and teach them throughout their lives continually, year after year, boost their self value. This way they will recognize the "joker" when he comes and not settle for the trick that comes with him. They need to know they have a great future ahead of them, and they can't let anyone get in their way of getting to their great destiny.

Once the Lord showed me all the triggers about myself that caused me to go after men, it brought me freedom. I vowed never again to go after men. It's hard sometimes, I won't lie, but with the help of God through prayer, He keeps me until the day He decides to send a man after me. It's just a matter of time. Until then i'm in line waiting for my turn to come.

chapter

NINE

Don't Do it!

Single Mothers on the M.O.V.E., don't ever turn your back on your child unless God almighty tells you to and if He does, its because He is taking over. Don't do it for anyone or anything. I don't care how many mistakes they make, or how many times you go around the same mountain with them.

If you are continually going around the same mountain with them, check and see what you can change within the order of your household. Evaluate your relationship between you, them and school making sure your involved in every way possible. Most of the time, a child is screaming from within and in need of someone to know how to reach them and deal with the area in their life that is troubling them. If you can't discern or understand what the problem is, then you need to ask the one who created them to show you. Ask God to let you know how to reach them. Sometimes our children walk around as if nothing is wrong with them, and all seems well, but don't be fooled.

There is always something to work on in their lives. We need to try to be aware of their emotional needs at all times. When finding out there is a problem, make the necessary changes to solve the problem and stick to it. Be consistent and you will see positive changes in your child.

I Did It

In this chapter I'm telling you don't do it, but let me tell you I did it. I temporarily gave up on my child to prove a point to my son. This section of this chapter is an "add-in" after just having a traumatizing 24 hour situation with my son. Ya'll, I was fed up. He was fifteen years old at the time (an adult now) and breaking away, trying to find himself, I guess. I don't know, but we had a problem.

I asked him to go outside and get his sister, because he wanted to go to the store and purchase football gear. Let me add that the sister he went to get is the one who puts up a fight over any and everything with him all the time. So, he came back angry and said, "Mom, Grace is not listening or coming, and she is hitting me and embarrassing me outside in front of all those people." Well, knowing her, she was doing just what he said she was doing. Since I wasn't ready to go right away, because I was still working on editing this book, I said to him, "Just give her a minute, she'll come in," and I knew she would, because she would start thinking about the trouble she would have with me if she did not. Well, that wasn't good enough for him. He slammed his fist on the table and said, "No, I want her to come now." I looked at him like he was crazy. Then he took the jacket he had on, slammed it on the floor, and said, "I'm going back out there and make her come." I knew that meant more trouble, so I said, "No, let her alone, she'll come." He said, "Man, I don't care, forget that—I'm going" and he stormed out the door. I got up, went to the door and calmly said "Come back here right now." Plus, ya'll know I did not want to be loud, yelling and carrying on with the neighbors listening. He kept going. I said, "You come back now, or you won't come back at all." Now keep in mind I'm getting tired, frustrated, and fed up with children. Well, he kept going, so I knew I had to put my word into action and show him who was the boss.

I went upstairs, packed his school books and some of his clothes in a duffel bag, put the bag in the car, and by the time he made it back with his sister, I was in the car waiting for him. (I was scared ya'll.) I told him to get in. He didn't know where we were going. When he got in, he said jokingly, "Who's in this bag?", and asked if it was my smallest daughter. I didn't laugh, and we were silent the whole way to his father's house. I pulled up into the driveway and said, "When you are ready to obey, be respectful, and listen to my words, call me and I will pick you up. There's your bag. Get out and go on in your dad's house." He gave me a thumbs up like it was all good, but I was hurting and so was he. (Please think twice before trying this at home, it could blow up in your face.)

As soon as he got out of the car and inside the house, I STARTED PRAYING!—praying that this plan would not go sour—praying in my most Holy faith, and in English, because all I wanted to do was set him straight and cause him to see that I was serious about him respecting me. Well, I'm going to tell you the enemy tried to get in my mind with thoughts of worry. I got home (still praying) and sat on the couch, and the question that came to me was, "Now what are you going to do?" I looked around the living room in desperation, and I spotted the follow-up ministry book from church where I kept phone numbers of first time visitors who had visited our church. I said to myself, "I'm going to do the work of the ministry, that's what I'm going to do. I'm going to carry on with God's business like nothing is the matter, and God will carry on with my business. I'll show the devil that he won't get the best of me or my son." So that's just what I did.

I began to call people and thank them for coming, invite them to come back again, and I would say a prayer with them. When I hung up that phone, I felt better. I continued praying throughout the night, but when I woke up the next morning, I said to myself, "I did it, I gave up on my son. What am I doing? I'm not a Single Mother on the M.O.V.E.! How can I publish this book now? I have messed up a whole chapter, spouting, "Don't do it." Little did I know, God was going to use this test I was going through as a testimony?

Long story short, I picked him up from his dad's for school the next morning (keeping the communication lines open between us). I prayed with him (keeping the communication lines open between us), told him I loved him and we missed him last night (keeping the communication lines open between us), took him out to breakfast, and offered to bring him lunch, while all at the same time letting him know he was welcome to come back when he was ready to obey, explaining to him that I wasn't trying to hurt him but he had to obey me, and not just totally ignore what I say to him.

He came back to our home after school. I said to him, "You should call your father and let him know you'll be there shortly." One hour went by and he did not call. I said "Why haven't you called your father? He needs to know where you are and when your coming." He looked hesitant. So, I said "Is there something you want to talk about?" He said, "I'm sorry. I want to obey you and listen to your words." I said, "Are you saying that because you want to stay at home, and he said, "Yes." I said, "I forgive you and I'm glad you're back at home."

The moral of the story is sometimes tough love works, but it can be really risky, especially if you're not a praying mother. I called a friend to pray with me before I went to bed the night I dropped him off at his fathers, I prayed most of the night, and then when I woke up the next morning, I called another friend to pray with me too. I wanted to call several other people the day it happened, but I would pick up the phone and hang it back up, because I was determined to trust God to bring me out of that one. Again—think twice before trying this at home.

Your The Parent

Ultimately, children follow their parents, so if we as parents would set the right example for them, we would see better results from their lives. If they are grown children, keep praying for them and speaking positive words about life to them and about them to others. Trust me, "All things are possible to him/her that believes."

God is almighty, and if we seek Him, He will talk to us about our children. He will tell us where to take them, where not to take them and leave them. He will reveal to us what to put them in and what not to put them in. Don't always go along with everything they want—children are just children. You have to show them that you know what's best for them, and you make the decisions of the household, not them.

Don't always go along with what other people say about them either. You know your child best, and if you don't, then you'd better start paying attention. Ask God what He wants for your child, and He will direct your path. If what He tells you lines up with the gifts and talents that you see in your child, then you know it is God speaking to you, and it's not just your idea or someone else's.

Make sure your child understands they have been placed on earth for a purpose, to do something that only they can do. Help them understand that no one else will be able to do that certain something like they can, because they are especially and uniquely made to do the job.

Teach your children to give to others, and don't always get them what they want. Say no sometimes, so they can learn the difference between a want and a need. Explain it to them. Our children need to be aware that there will always be someone who has more than or less than them. They need to know that they are who they are and no one can change them but God, and that who they are is okay for now. You need to tell them not to be jealous of or want to be like someone else, just to strive to become a better them. Be realistic with them and let them know that in life there will be hard times they will have to face. When they do face hard times, if we teach them as much as we can and prepare them properly, they should get through those hard times easily. We should definitely teach them to pray, study the Bible, go to church, and exercise self-control, on top of many other things they will need to get through those hard times—things like never give up, keep pressing even though it hurts—you know, stuff like that.

It is important to bond with your children and let them know that family is second only to God in importance. Don't create fale relitives like cousins, brothers, and sisters that are not truly related to them, because when they grow up and see that those people will go on with their lives without them, they will really see who is still there, and those are the people who are truly family. So, I teach my children not to go against one another or another relative outside our immediate family, because they will always be there for you when nobody else is. You know you can always call your cousin or somebody in the family if you choose.

Most importantly our children need to know that God loves them. Jesus died on the cross for them to be free from all sinful acts and to be free to do what is right. All they have to do is believe in Him, ask Him into their little hearts, and talk to Him daily through prayer. I assure you, they will lead much better lives.

It is our responsibility as parents to teach them the right way because when we stand before God on judgment day, He may ask us why we didn't train them up in the way they should go, so that when they got older, they would not depart from Him or the truth. What will your answer be?

chapter

TEN

Is It Right? Or Wrong?

We all have gray areas in our lives. You know those areas that aren't black or white, right or wrong, but just there. Those areas that we never really stop to think about or we seem to have a hard time concluding whether they be right or wrong for us. We continue right along with doing these gray things in our lives never considering if God is pleased with our actions. Usually we tend to put these areas of our life off until tomorrow hoping they work themselves out.This could be your weight, maybe you continually over eat and it's causing you to get larger and larger putting your health at risk, maybe it's a relationship that your in that you need to get out of because it's not bringing forth good fruit in you and your children's life, maybe it's just plain laziness day after day that results in your house work not being complete, the bible does say Godliness is cleanliness. It could also be your attitude towards people, maybe negative, backbiting, gossiping ways that you have and not notice. Have you ever stopped to look at yourself and say "God what in my life or about me are you displeased with?" It's called self examination. I mean really itemize the areas in your life, I know you think your perfectly fine, but I challenge you to ask God what He would like you to change, start, stop or get rid of and see what He says.

What we want is to let these areas alone in our life, we want to do what we want to do, because it feels good to our flesh or we are too lazy to do what we need to do to make things right. Single Mothers on the M.O.V.E., never run, or passively ignore correcting areas in their life. They stand firm and face to face with the issues at hand and deal with them until the correction is made, no matter how bad it hurts. Understand you will never be perfect until you go to be with God in heaven, but while on earth God wants us to never quit working toward perfecting areas of our life.

Seeing The Truth About You Helps

I remember I was going through a time in my life where I felt I wanted to do absolutely nothing for anyone, anymore, but my children and myself and I felt like I just did not want to be bothered with people, because people will drain you if you let them. I was given an opportunity to move into a particular residential location, but because I knew I tend to be a nice and kind individual to people and of course as a Christian we are expected to be kind, it was difficult sometimes for me to say no, until I learned that no is not a bad word (thanks Pastor Dixon). So, I said, "I can't move over there, because I know people over there will just drain me." So there was another residential space coming available in the same complex, but I would have had to wait 6 more months for it. I told the renters I said I'll just wait. Because, I knew if I waited for that particular place there would not be many people in that area that would bother me (so I thought). But, then God said to me "how is that loving your neighbor as yourself, Jesus didn't run from people He helped people". "BUSTED"! I said "ok God forgive me." He said "you just need to learn how to set up boundaries, if you can help them today help them if you can't just say "no," don't let their faces, or what you think they may be thinking about you push you into doing what you can't do, and if they like you they like you and if they don't they don't, but always be willing to help others? I became more courageous and bold in my speech, and in a nice way did what I had to do, when I had to do it! I did end up moving in the very place I was avoiding, it took some time of opening up to those who had needs but slowly and gradually I opened up more and more and before you know I was reaching out to them praying with them letting their children sleep over at my house (and thats not always easy when you have your own children to deal with), taking them to church and helping in everyway I could. This was a process of healing that I aloud God to take me through with people. I can tell you this process did hurt and some days I was like "oh no", but I prayed and said "God help me to love, open up, relax more and help me say no when I need to say no". This was an issue that I was dealt with because I had become hard toward people around me, because of misuse I've experienced throughout the years. I wanted to ignore it all and just say "this is just who I am and I don't care what anyone says", but I deciced not to do that, because I cared what God thought of me.

Write down one by one where you can improve things in your life, write down strategies of how you will improve, and then seek necessary tools for improvement. It may be in the form of a book from the library or bookstore, a teaching tape/cd series from someone with expertise in the particular area where you want and need improvement, it could be a class, or counsel from a Godly person like a Pastor, mentor, teacher or someone whose opinion you value.

I recommend you get out a Bible and seek answers within that as well and if its weight loss you seek keep an eye out at www.lashandafaye.info for my next book "From Fat to Fabulous". You'll also find encouraging notes for single mothers, weightloss, relationships and all sorts of other things. You may only be able to work on one thing at a time. That's okay as long as you are **ongoing** with improving yourself. Single Mothers on the M.O.V.E. deal with every issue in their lives!

chapter

ELEVEN

Take Care Of yourself

Single Mother, take care of you! Take care of yourself physically, mentally, and spiritually. We Single Mothers have to live a long time. We have our children to take care of and steer them into adulthood. We want to see our grandchildren, great grandchildren, and great great grandchildren, we want to live a life of longevity to do all the things we've dreamed of; this means we must take care of ourselves.

The first thing a Single Mother on the M.O.V.E. should do to take care of herself is take care of her body. You can do this through eating properly. Find out how different types of food effect the inside of your bodily organs. By eating the right foods your body will continue working properly; don't just stop at finding out what they are, buy them and incorporate them into your daily eating habits so that your body gets the proper nutrients it needs to live a healthy and long life

It was hard for me to change my daily eating habits and begin purchasing healthier food items. Not so much that it was difficult for me, but for my children they would complain and complain until I would just give in and go back to purchsing so many of the unhealthy, sugary, salty snacks, the processed food items that are already cooked and all we have to do is pop it in the microwave/oven. You all know what i'm talking about. It has been easier to buy food already prepared than to buy the fresh foods, clean them, marinate them and cook them. The problem with that is those foods are filled with sodium and all types of additives and preservatives and they barely give our bodies the nutrients we need. Let's get back to the old way, natural way, or as some would say a more time consuming way of doing things when it comes to cooking. This way believe it or not is the healthier way of doing things.

Daily exercise is also a must. If you're not engaging in some sort of daily exercise, then it's hard to classify yourself as a Single Mother on the M.O.V.E. Single Mothers on the M.O.V.E. are **motivated**, and when someone is motivated, she demonstrates her motivation by actions. Exercise is an action word as well as an action. Unless you have a medically sound excuse for not getting physically fit, you should have a daily exercise regimen. If you are not exercising in some capacity in your life, you are not going to be in the best health that you can be for you or your children. Be your children's example of what a healthy lifestyle looks like.

Mothers, we need to take care of our bodies on the outside, so that we can be as beautiful on the outside as we are on the inside. Amen? Care about your hair, care about how you smell, care about your clothing. All these things are important. If you don't care about you, then it will teach your children not to care about themselves.

I remember when I was in a place of depression, and I would barely comb my hair and brush my teeth. I would wait all day to shower, and, some days, not shower at all. I was home all day because I didn't have a job, just taking care of the children. I only had one child in school at the time, so I would do what was necessary for him just to go to school and not for the rest of us.

One day, when I was expecting them to care for themselves properly and they were not, the Lord showed me that it was because I wasn't teaching or modeling it properly for them. How could I expect something from them that I wasn't giving them? From that point on, I began to work on myself and model good hygiene habits.

My mother taught me good habits, but life beat me down to the place where I just couldn't see hope on a daily basis. At one point, I couldn't see past where I was heading into my future I didn't believe there would be something better coming, all I could see is where I was. Where had all my childhood dreams, visions and motivations gone to? What I found out was that I needed to act like I could see then even though I could not. I needed to believe something good was coming although I didn't know what, and expect it until it shows up. Sometimes when good did come I had such a negative outlook I couldn't even recognize it, life can get you down like that sometimes, but I'm writing you to say RISE UP GIRL, RISE UP THERE IS A BETTER DAY COMING, THIS TOO SHALL PASS!

Another component to Single Mothers caring for themselves, is definitely spiritual awareness, involvment and guidance. We are human beings, but we are also spiritual beings. The human side of us is that part of us that we can look into the mirror and see. The spiritual part is the part that lives inside of your body and looks out of your eyes into the world around you. This part of you can't be seen with the natural eye.

Realize that God is a Spirit. The Bible says He created us (you and me) in His image and likeness. God is three beings in one: God the creator (or master mind); God the Holy Spirit which is God on earth right now here to identify with us as a spirit being ; and God the Son, Jesus, who was a man created by God, sent to earth as in a body to identify with us as we are in bodily form. Jesus was put inside of a clean woman who had never had sex with a man before. He grew for nine months and was then born into the world and lived 33 years. God called Him the Savior of the world.

How awesomely, miraculous is that! I haven't heard of anyone else having a baby without having sex, have you? Every time I think about how he was created i'm in awe. To top it all off, the Man died, was buried in a tomb for three days, and still God rose Him up from death, he actually defeated death and anything related to it. He lived and walked the earth again until he literally was seen going up into the sky by human eyes. All this, the Bible tells us, He did for you and me to save us from our sins and give us eternal life in heaven after we die and leave this earth. What we have to do is believe it and accept it.

Forget about the Bible for a second and do a historical research on Jesus, and you will find that this is true. Don't take my word; don't even take the Bible's word. Research it the historical way and see what you come up with. Then compare it to the Bible and I know you'll believe what the Bible says. The Bible has sold more copies in the history of book selling than any other book ever written. I wonder why? It says in **John 3:16:**

"For God so greatly loved and dearly prized the world that He [even] gave up His only begotten ([a]unique) Son, so that whoever believes in (trusts in, clings to, relies on) Him shall not perish (come to destruction, be lost) but have eternal (everlasting) life."

As I said before, God is Spirit, God is a Man (Jesus), and The Creator, and He created us. The first thing we should do to take care of ourselves spiritually is connect to The Father, God, through Jesus Christ. You can do this by simply praying, asking Jesus to forgive you of the sins you have been practicing on a daily basis, believe that He died for you on the cross (watch the movie "The Passion of the Christ" to get a visual of what He did for you) and that God raised him from the dead for you, and ask Him to come into your heart be your savior and change you. Next I would encourage you to start reading the bible to recognize what God loves, and what he hates, because God has certain standards that He expects us to live up to and when we learn them and ask him for help with meeting those standards, he will gradually change you.

It's just that simple, and that is the beginning of caring for you spiritually. If you prayed a prayer similar to that just now, please log onto www.lashandafaye.info share that information with me, we are now sisters in Christ! It doesn't stop there, of course. We must also fellowship (keep company) with people that have accepted Jesus in their hearts as well. This means we should go to church on a regular basis to meet new believers like us. We also need to hear new teaching from the pastor about Jesus and God's ways. This way we can grow and stay strong spiritually. I encourage you to begin visiting church's until you find one that you are comfortable with.

We Single Mothers also need to talk to God on a daily basis. This is basic praying, essential to staying sane....lol and caring for ourselves. Be real with God; tell Him the truth. He already knows everything anyway. The bible says He knows our thought before we speak them. WOW! We can't hide anything form him. Be open and transparent with Him. This will help you get rid of bad habits much more quickly than not discussing them at all.

Get a good Bible that you can understand and read daily. Also, take it to church with you when you go. Your walk with God is personal. He has a lot to talk with you about, so run after Him and walk with Him daily.

Last, but not least, take care of yourself emotionally. If you do what I have shared with you already on a regular basis, then this area of caring for yourself will be half way accomplished. We need to take time out for ourselves, Single Mothers. I'm talking about a vacation away from it all. A time when we can relax our mind and emotions. Every year since 2005, God has blessed me to go away for one week, or four days at the least. Sometimes it has been with the children and sometimes without.

Drop it all and get away from everything and everybody. I recommend incorporating spiritual things into this vacation if at all possible. I've been places like Florida, Ohio and Georgia to Christian conferences and I left the children behind. I really enjoyed the Mega Fest sponsored by Bishop TD and Serita Jakes and the Potter's House family. I attended two years in a row, and every time I went I was changed. I'm revived in every way. I get built up in the Lord, I get time away from the children, and I get my emotional needs taken care of. Don't be afraid to get away. Just make sure you are leaving the children with people who can be trusted!

What ever you do single mother, take care of you!

chapter

TWELVE

Are You a Giver or a Taker?

Being a giver is important as a single mother. It has been my experience throughout life that giving makes room for you and your children to receive. As a child, I saw my mother, a single mother herself, give tremendously. She gave constantly. There were times when she would buy everybody she knew, children and adults, Christmas gifts year after year. She gave money to people who needed help throughout their life. She would buy groceries for people and give all our good clothing that we had outgrown to children who were in need.

She was just a constant giver, and when I grew up and began to form a relationship with the Lord, the Holy Spirit spoke to me one day and said, "The reason you always have your needs met and people are always giving to you is because of your mother's giving. When you were a child, all of her giving was storing up treasures in heaven with me so that later on, when I saw that you had a need, I remembered your mothers giving and supplied your need based on her giving."

I was so amazed; all I could say was, "Wow! Thank you, Jesus, and I thank you, mom."

Giving will not only sustain your children, but it will also sustain you. If you are a giver, then God will make sure you have everything you need. The scripture in Luke 6:38 that comes to mind. It simply states,

"If you give, you will receive. Your gift will return to you in full measure, pressed down, shaken together to make room for more and running over. Whatever measure you use in giving, large or small, it will be used to measure what is given back to you" (NLT)

God also tells us in the bible that we should give a tenth of our earnings a tenth is a tithe which is 10% of your pay check, if your check is $100 God is saying give $10 to the local church, or if you don't have a church that you attend yet, give it to your local homeless shelter. Jesus wants us to help those who are less fortunate than us. When you get a church that you like and you begin to attend on a regular basis then give your 10% to the church, remember the church has bills to pay. The water we use to wash our hands and flush the toilet, the lights we use to see when were inside, the toilet paper and paper towels we need, communion, and I could go on and on so never think churches just want your money they need it to survive just like you do at home. Nothing but good comes out of giving for you in the long run, remember that.

It's also good when you're giving to people, special friends , or organizations that you support. When giving to friends give something appropriate to the occasion or find out what that they want, or need before giving to them if you can, because you don't know what's going on in their organization or life. They could be in need of just a simple Grocery Store gift card for food, and personal hygiene products and your going out buying a new Television, or clothing and thats not what they have need of. Of course they are going to be thankful and I'm sure they will appreciate what you have given them, but all the whole time they may be thinking I need some food; it's better if you can hit that special place where they have a need than to get them what you want or think they need.

Make sure your connected to the right people because some people are just takers and not givers; they will suck up everything you give your time, money, gifts and talents and never give back to you, or when you ask them for something they say "oh I can't because of this or that, but when they needed you, you were always there for them". Do you have people like that in your life? If so, make sure you set up boundries with them and in some cases you may even have to cut them off because they are just out for themselves. If you are giving someone a surprise, try and get some one to find out for you what that person has need of, or take the time out of your busy life and spend time with them, listening and getting to know them in order to find out who they are and what they enjoy. Spending time with an individual will help you see what's going on in their life.

So, if you are a giver, be a good giver (give all the time, plan you're giving, and give wisely). Be free in giving, give with a willing heart, without doubt or hesitation unless you know In your heart this is not the time for you to give, then don't give; otherwise be a cheerful giver. God was a good giver He gave His best His only begotten Son (don't give away your worse stuff or something you wouldn't want someone to give to you or your children; give your best). If you do this, you and your children will always be blessed.

Conclusion

Overall, it takes a lot of work being a Single Mother, but with God on your side, perseverance, discipline, and consistency, you can do it.

Following are some statistics and characteristics that **do not** reflect a Single Mother on the M.O.V.E. child:

Children from fatherless homes are twice as likely to be high school dropouts.

Ninety percent of all homeless and runaway children are from fatherless homes

Seventy-one percent of all high school dropouts come from fatherless homes

Seventy-five percent of all adolescent patients in chemical abuse centers come from fatherless homes

Fatherless children have more emotional and behavioral problems.

Girls from fatherless homes are three times as likely to be unwed teenage mothers.

Boys from fatherless homes have higher incidents of unemployment, incarceration, and noninvolvement with their own children.

Ninety-five percent of all violent crime is committed by men from single mother homes*

*Info found at website betterdads.net.

These are statistics of children in single parent households. All though these statistics are true for some children, I declare this will not be true for our children they don't have to end up like this. These are the plans and strategies of the enemy (the devil) his job is to kill, steal, and destroy our children, God wants our children to have a good and abundant life, so if we continue in the ways of God and apply the right disciplined strategies to our children's life we can have victorious children.

Special Thanks

    I want to start with giving thanks to God the father, God the Son, and God the Holy Spirit. Jesus Christ, who is my Lord and my Savior I thank Him for calling me out of darkness into his marvelous light, for creating in me a clean heart and renewing a right spirit within me daily. I thank Him for giving me the gift of writing and allowing me to share it with the world to bring hope, salvation, peace, deliverance and healing; I thank him for creating an audience that is interested in reading what I have written, and for making what I do a success.

    I want to give thanks to my mother (CaSandra Coleman) for having me and raising me with a stern, strict hand and a touch of class and excellence. Thanks to my stepfather Larry Hodges for being there for me throughout my life even after the divorce from my mother. Thanks to my biological father Larry Collins for your participation with my mother that caused me to come into this world and thanks for reaching out to me in my latter years of adulthood.

    Thanks to my late pastors Reverend and Sister Fritz of New Mount Calvary Baptist Church who first took me to church in Lansing Mi. to my former pastors, Reverend & Sister Clayton, of the New Mount Calvary Baptist Church in Lansing, Michigan, who watched over my soul until I was eighteen years old and decided to depart from the church.

    Thanks to the Tabernacle of David Church, formally Pentecostal Outreach, under the leadership of Pastor & First Lady Trice, where, when I was just a third grader while visiting there on a regular basis with my babysitter Dyrese, I was first introduced to shouting, dancing, lifting my hands to the Lord, and just praising his name radically. It was their where first felt the power of God.

Thanks to Reverend Paul & First Lady Garret, of Mt. Olive Full Gospel Church, in Lansing, Michigan, who watched over my soul for a brief time as I was trying to find my way back to the Lord.

Thanks to Pastor & First Lady Stephens, of Life Christian Church, in Lansing, Michigan, they really displayed the love of God in action to me for the first time. Through Pastor Stephens actions of love he taught me that all white people were not the same because until that point of my life, I had a pre-conceived idea about all white people and I did not like them very much, but God was able to change my perception through being in that ministry for a short period.

Thanks to Pastor & First Lady Cox, of Mount Hope Church in the City, in Lansing, Michigan, who briefly watched over my soul as I was continuing to get closer to God and find my way. It was there that I learned about helping others and reaching out to the poor and homeless.

Thanks to Pastor Dave & Mary Joe Williams, of Mount Hope Church, in Lansing, Michigan, who watched over my soul as a regular attendee for 1 year. It was there where I learned that God has so much more to offer than the world's way of doing things. I learned that God is a funny God, a big God, and a simple God.

Thank to my pastors of 2 ½ years, Pastors James and Stacia Pierce, who watched over my soul at a time when I was just tore up from the floor up. I was in a slump, and all I remember is being encouraged, motivated, and taught that I can have what God has for me, and what He has is the best, not the rest. I remember the day I got my joy back while being ministered to at a woman in the word bible study; I was revived in that ministry. Thank you again, Dr. James & Dr. Stacia Pierce.

I have to give thanks to another one of Gods great man and woman of God who watched over my soul when I got out of the perfect will of God and got into the permissive will of God, taking a brief break of nine months (somebody say just enough time for a new birthing) from my home pastors Ronnie and Corintia Calhoun. Deciding to leave I went to Dr. Phillip E. & Dr. Patricia A. Owens' church, of The Emmanuel

Temple Community Church, in Lansing Michigan. A big thank you to you all for watching over my soul while I was in the permissive will of God. Thank you for the ministry of deliverance which shook some demons right up out of me.

I can't forget what I call my "still away vacation" Pastors they don't know me but I sure do know and Love them. Thank you Bishop T. D. & First Lady Sarita Jakes. I have attened the Mega Fest a couple times and my life has changed for the better. I watch the television broadcast and stream online services. Whenever I can and every time you open your mouth for the Lord Bishop something changes in my life I can never get through a sermon without tears flowing. When ever I attended the Mega Fest and returned home I saw clearer than I did before I went. I was challenged, revived, re-established in the faith and made ready to continue into destiny. I'm thankful that when I've been their my spirit has never been tainted I've only ran into wholesome, clean, Godly experiences during my visit and I thank God for that.

Thanks to my former Pastors who watched over my soul from 2000-2008. Dr. Ronnie & Dr. Corinthia Calhoun. For 8years of my life (with an exception of the nine months I attended Emmanuel's Temple), I was a part of the ministry of Purpose Outreach Revival Center, in Lansing Michigan. Where they taught me true worship.

They freely allowed our congregation to praise and worship until we entered into Gods presence and received breakthrough. They were and still reamain living examples of no nonsense and no compromise life styles in God. They constantly refer us to the word of God for help. They teach that it's there and only there where we find all of what we need. It would take a whole book to write of all that God has given to me through the lifestyle and ministry of God in them. Truly they are a man and woman of God. Thank you again Pastor Ronnie and Evangelist Corinthia Calhoun I Love You.

Thank you to Pastor and Minister Dixon of Abundant Grace Faith Church who so lovingly took me in and watched over my soul as a member from 2009-2011 until I departed from the city of Lansing. Pastor and Minister Dixon is truly a man and woman of faith, family and love and I was strengthened in all of those areas while attending that ministry. I will never forget the true love and accecptance that Abundant Grace Faith showed to my family and I!

Let me also thank some of my VIP mentors: Kristine Urbauer, the late Isha Smith, Minister Michael Venya, Sister Sharon Dade Daniels, my University English/writing instructor Chris Miller of Davenport University in Lansing, Michigan, and my good friend Shanell Henry A.K.A Gospel Rap Artist "Mizz Reality". Until this point in my life, these were/ are people that invested quality time into my life. Had I not opened up to them and if they had not taken the time to talk with me, minister to me, listen to me, and teach me, I can honestly say I don't know if I would have made it this far.

I Love You All, and Thank You!

Thank you for reading this book in its entirety. I want to hear feedback from you about this book, how the book affected you. Please buy the book to give to other single mothers out of the ten million single mothers in America I want to get this book into the hands of one million, help me do that.

Please go to www.lashandafaye.info place your comments online, contact us and join our email mailing list to receive periodic messages from LaShanda.